REACHING FOR THE STARS

JIM CARREY
Funny man

Joan Wallner

Published by Abdo & Daughters, 4940 Viking Drive, Suite 622, Edina, Minnesota 55435.

Copyright © 1996 by Abdo Consulting Group, Inc., Pentagon Tower, P.O. Box 36036, Minneapolis, Minnesota 55435 USA. International copyrights reserved in all countries. No part of this book may be reproduced in any form without written permission from the publisher.

Printed in the United States.

Cover Photo credit: Wide World Photos
Interior Photo credits: Wide World Photos, page 21
                    Archive Photos, pages 5, 7, 15, 24, 25, 27

Edited by Rosemary Wallner

Library of Congress Cataloging-in-Publication Data

Wallner, Joan.
Jim Carrey : funny man / Joan Wallner.
    p. cm. — (Reaching for the stars)
     ISBN 1-56239-522-X
1. Carrey, Jim, 1962- . 2. Comedians—United States—Biography-
Juvenile literature. 3. Motion picture actors and actresses-
-United States—Biography—Juvenile literature. I. Title. II . Series.
PN2287.C278W35   1995
791.43'028'092—dc20
[B]   95-22136
                                         CIP
                                         AC

TABLE OF CONTENTS

RUBBERY, FUNNY, AND CREATIVE 4

GROWING UP MAKING FACES 6

A CHILDHOOD WITH LITTLE MONEY 9

FIRST DEBUT AT A COMEDY CLUB 11

CREATING A CAREER 12

TAKING HIS FACE TO THE STATES 14

CHANGING HIS ACT 17

MOVIE BREAKS 18

A BIG BREAK 20

TURNING POINT 23

MORE ADVENTURES 28

TV SHOWS AND MOVIES (1984-1995) 30

JIM CARREY'S ADDRESS 31

RUBBERY, FUNNY, AND CREATIVE

Reporters have been interviewing Jim Carrey ever since he appeared in movies and on TV shows in the late 1980s. Here's how some have described this talented actor and comedian:

- "Multi-jointed, flexi-faced comic."—*Newsweek* magazine.

- "There's a nasty verve to Carrey's humor, a surrealism that kids love."—*Saturday Night* magazine.

- "Handsome and charming."—*Seventeen* magazine.

- "The man with the Silly Putty face."—*Scripps Howard News Service.*

In the first eight years of his comedy career, Carrey did stand-up performances all across North America and appeared in five movies. After his astonishing face-altering creations on the TV show "In Living Color," Carrey's career grew. In the next four years, he appeared in four movies. Those films included *Ace Ventura: Pet Detective*, *The Mask* and *Dumb and Dumber*.

"Just let me do what I do and everything will be fine," Carrey said about creating astonishing and goofy movie characters.

What does Carrey think about all the publicity and fame he's found since his first movie roles? In a 1994 interview, he told one reporter that even if he lost his fame and fortune, it would be okay. Why? Because he only has one real need: to make people laugh.

Jim Carrey plays limousine driver Lloyd Christmas in the hit comedy,
Dumb and Dumber.

GROWING UP MAKING FACES

Jim Eugene Carrey was born January 17, 1962, in Newmarket, Ontario, Canada. He lived in Aurora, a town just north of Toronto, with his parents, two older sisters and brother. Carrey's father, Percy, gave up a career playing jazz saxophone music for accounting work in Toronto. Carrey's mother, Kathleen, was a homemaker.

As a child, Carrey lived in many Canadian towns, which is where he learned to make his family laugh. While eating in his high chair, Carrey innocently began what would become his comedy career. At first, he simply twisted his mouth, eyes, nose, and ears to create many different faces. His family laughed at the faces he made.

As Carrey grew older, his family demanded more funny faces. Carrey remembers a night when he was three years old. His father ran into his room with wide eyes and waving his arms. "Jim! Jim!" his father cried. "Sorry to wake you, but your mom and I could use a good laugh." Asking for a little song and dance, Mr. Carrey said, "What do you think we make you sleep in tap shoes for?"

Jim Carrey puts on his famous grin in the movie Dumb and Dumber.

People who didn't live at the Carrey house, however, only saw Carrey as a shy, withdrawn boy. But then his family moved to Toronto when Carrey was eight years old. While in the schoolyard with his classmates, Carrey made a face. Like magic, the other children laughed.

"I really didn't have any friends or anything like that," Carrey said. But when he made a zany-looking face, "I had tons of friends. That was when I broke out of my shell at school."

Growing up, Carrey's heroes were comedians such as Dick Van Dyke, Jackie Gleason and, a little later, Steve Martin. Carrey discovered he could make friends by acting out all the "wild stuff that was going on in my head," just like real comedians do.

Carrey not only entertained classmates in the schoolyard, but also in the classroom. Carrey was a good student and often finished his work before others. He would then entertain other students who were not finished. One day, a teacher caught Carrey clowning around. She asked Carrey to come to the front of the class and show everyone what he was doing. He did and the students loved it. The teacher let Carrey entertain his classmates at the end of class, so his humor wouldn't disrupt them. Then one day, the teacher asked Carrey to do his act at the holiday school play.

For the play, Carrey did a Three Stooges act. Glancing at the school's principal, Sister Mary Joan, he saw her on her hands and knees in a fit of laughter. From that moment on, comedy was the only thing he could think of doing. "Acting goofy became my entire motivation for living," Carrey said.

A CHILDHOOD WITH LITTLE MONEY

The laughter came to a temporary halt when Carrey was 13. After 35 years as an accountant, Mr. Carrey lost his job. He was 51 years old and couldn't find work. The Carrey's had little money and couldn't afford the house they were living in, so they lived in their van. The Carrey's also lived for a while in a tent in King City, Ontario, in the front yard of Carrey's eldest sister. "We were basically drifting," Carrey said.

His parents finally found work as janitors at a truck rim factory in Toronto. But they still didn't have enough money to buy a house or live comfortably. Along with two of his three siblings, thirteen-year-old Carrey began working at the factory.

As he grew older, he worked more hours at night and went to school during the day. Because he was working eight hours after school, Carrey said he often slept at school. "I went from being a top student in the class to 'I don't understand a word you're saying,'" Carrey said. He also became very angry and had no friends.

Eventually, Carrey couldn't work and go to school. When he was in tenth grade, he had to quit school to help his family make money. "I know how family problems affect teenagers," Carrey said. "If it's bad at home, you ain't got an easy deal."

FIRST DEBUT AT
A COMEDY CLUB

Carrey could have stopped laughing altogether because of his family's problems. But he didn't. He focused his attention on making his family laugh during the difficult times. Laughing, he found, also made him feel better.

So Carrey made faces and told jokes once again. Being a jokester himself, Mr. Carrey liked his son's humor and was his biggest supporter.

"He [Mr. Carrey] was completely nuts," Carrey said about his father. Carrey described his dad as someone who would put a stocking over his head and run out of the garage when you pulled up in the car.

Mr. Carrey surprised his 15-year-old son one day with the news that he had scheduled a performance at a comedy club called Yuk Yuk's in Toronto. For the first time, Carrey would be performing on stage in front of strangers. Carrey was excited.

To prepare for the performance, Mrs. Carrey told her son to wear a yellow polyester suit because all the other men were wearing them. She assured him the suit would be stunning because all the guests on the TV talk show "The Phil Donahue Show" wore them. Clad in polyester, Carrey went to Yuk Yuk's for his debut as a young comic.

Carrey recalled the club as if it were yesterday. He said the club looked like two lanes of a bowling alley with a stage at the end of it. It had old chairs and tables with the hippest crowd waiting for a good laugh.

The stand-up was a disaster. The crowed booed him off the stage. "I don't even remember what I talked about," said Carrey. "Mostly I did impressions."

CREATING A CAREER

Growing up with little money, little home stability, and at times with few friends, Carrey knew success wouldn't be any easier. But he didn't give up after his failure at the club. He spent the next two years preparing for another stand-up show at Yuk Yuk's. And with a more polished show, 17-year-old Carrey auditioned for Mark Breslin, the owner of the club. Breslin signed up Carrey to perform his second debut. The performance was a success, and Breslin asked Carrey to perform more shows. Carrey began practicing different impersonations all the time for his show. Before testing his new face in front of an audience, he would practice alone.

Carrey often hid himself inside a walk-in closet for hours, twisting his face in front of a mirror. He wanted to make sure he could impersonate someone perfectly.

Asked how he can twist his face, Carrey said, "Because I tried."

Still in his teens, Carrey lived for a while in Jackson's Point on the southern shore of Lake Simcoe. As his success grew, he moved to Walmer Road in Toronto. His parents moved in with him.

Within two years, Carrey was one of the most popular comedy stars in Toronto. Audiences jammed comedy clubs to see the man known as the "rubber-faced" man.

Carrey could do a hundred impersonations by altering his face, voice, and body. Driving himself to different clubs throughout Canada in his Volkswagon bug, Carrey got his first big break. Veteran critic Bruce Blackadar of the *Toronto Star* saw Carrey's stand-up act in 1981. Blackadar wrote a rave review saying that in five years, Carrey would become as big as comedians Johnny Carson or Richard Pryor.

TAKING HIS FACE TO THE STATES

Carrey realized his act went as far as it could in Canadian comedy clubs. In 1981, Blackadar's review moved Carrey into the spotlight. At age 19, Carrey packed up and headed to Los Angeles for an appearance on "The Tonight Show." Carrey also performed at Mitzi Shore's Comedy Store in Hollywood. The club is where comedians such as David Letterman and Robin Williams performed before they became stars. Carrey was a sensation from the moment he stepped on stage.

Jim Carrey in full costume for the movie The Mask.

Instead of making impersonations he knew how to do, Carrey took a chance. He asked the audience who they wanted to see. When they told him, he altered his face, voice, and body instantly before the crowd. The people were in awe of his abilities.

Comedian Louie Anderson, who saw Carrey at the club, said Carrey is "probably the best impressionist there ever was." Ron Scribner, a former co-manager of Carrey's, said Carrey "absolutely devastated crowds."

Carrey gained popularity and familiarity with other comedians. Rodney Dangerfield was so impressed by Carrey that he asked Carrey to go on tour with him. Carrey did, and that led to an opening act for singer Andy Williams and a TV special with comedian Rich Little.

But Carrey wanted to be known for more than his impersonation abilities. Carrey said he wanted people to see him as a comic, not just a good impersonator. He wanted to do things that had never been done before.

CHANGING HIS ACT

Friends warned Carrey that changing his act could ruin his career because people knew him only for his impersonations. Carrey told himself that if he failed, it couldn't be worse than the difficult times he had as a child. "I had to try," Carrey said about taking the risk of failure. So he set out to prove to himself that he could change his act.

First he stopped impersonating celebrities and famous people on stage. He then turned down a second appearance on "The Tonight Show." Carrey took himself out of the spotlight to prepare his new comedian image. Canadians who had flocked to see Carrey at comedy clubs now heard little about the "rubber-faced" man. The only news they heard was that he was living with 37-year-old singer Linda Ronstadt in 1983. But the relationship didn't last. "I broke up with her because she was too young for me," the 21-year-old Carrey said jokingly.

Carrey enrolled in an acting class. In 1984, he landed a role in his first TV show, NBC's "The Duck Factory."

But the show dropped in ratings and was canceled in its first season. Carrey knew that he could go back to doing on-stage impersonations, but he didn't. He was ready for Hollywood and the movies.

MOVIE BREAKS

When "The Duck Factory" was canceled, Carrey was just beginning to reveal his talents as a comedian. Carrey was hired for a minor movie role in the 1984 comedy *Finders Keepers*. The movie is about a mistaken identity and a stolen fortune.

In 1985, he starred with Lauren Hutton in *Once Bitten*, a movie about a naive young man under the control of a beautiful, middle-aged vampire.

His biggest role to date came in 1986. Carrey landed a supporting role in *Peggy Sue Got Married*, starring Kathleen Turner and Nicholas Cage. Carrey played one of Cage's high school friends.

On stage at comedy clubs, Carrey's act was taking shape. People liked the new Carrey act, which had a reputation for being bizarre. He talked directly to his audience about life's problems. Doing something new each night became Carrey's goal.

While performing in a comedy club, Carrey met Melissa Womer, an actress from Altoona, Pennsylvania. She was working as a waitress at the club.

In March 1986, Carrey and Womer were married. The following year, they had a baby girl, Jane.

Carrey's life continued to improve. Carrey showed his rubber-face in Clint Eastwood's *The Dead Pool* in 1988. He played Johnny Squares, a rock star. Given the chance to select the song he would lip-sync to, Carrey selected "Welcome to the Jungle," by the then unfamiliar band Guns n' Roses. "I made them what they are today," Carrey said of the band's success.

In 1989, Carrey created a much bigger role in *Earth Girls Are Easy*. He played one of three aliens who land their disabled spaceship in the backyard of a Valley girl's home, played by Geena Davis.

During those five years, Carrey's popularity increased. It was then that producers who were creating a new Fox sitcom TV show saw Carrey's comedy. They wanted him for their show.

A BIG BREAK

Carrey was faced with a big decision in 1990. That year, the producers of "In Living Color" asked him to perform on their prime-time TV sitcom. Carrey wanted to act in movies, as he had been doing. Performing in a TV sitcom wasn't what he really wanted to do. "But that show was too good a chance to pass up," he remembered.

The show featured eleven black performers and two white performers, Carrey and Kelly Coffield. "Being the only white guy, [the other actors] rode me a bit," Carrey said about the beginning of the sitcom. "But I'd [joke with them] right back." Carrey became known as the "rubber-faced white guy."

Jim Carrey (bottom right) with the comedy team from the hit television show "In Living Color."

It was during his seasons on the Emmy-nominated show that millions of people saw Carrey's true talents. Putting his mind to work, Carrey created dozens of characters between 1990 and 1994. He created Body Builder Vera de Milo, who swallowed a few too many steroid pills. He also created Fire Marshall Bill, an out-of-control firefighter who issued handy home-safety tips.

His friend and costar Damon Wayans once said that Carrey is one of few performers no comic wanted to follow on stage. "'In Living Color' was such a fun show to do," Carrey said. "I got the license to do what I wanted."

The role led to Showtime's "Jim Carrey's Unnatural Act" in November 1991, and to a role in Fox's Emmy-nominated TV show "Doing Time on Maple Drive" in 1992. "Maple Drive" was about a happy suburban family with one son who is secretly a homosexual, and another who is an alcoholic. Carrey played the son with the drinking problem.
In 1993, his TV career was doing well. But Carrey was ready to work on something new. He had already said yes to two comedy movies: *Ace Ventura: Pet Detective* and *The Mask*.

TURNING POINT

The public first saw *Ace Ventura: Pet Detective* in February 1994. In the film, Carrey played a detective who rescues the team mascot of the Miami Dolphins.

"I had so much fun doing the role," Carrey said about playing the detective. He also saw his career jump into the spotlight, along with the success of the film. The movie was rated number one when it was released and earned $72 million at the box office.

In his next movie, *The Mask*, Carrey played Stanley Ipkiss, an average guy who finds an ancient mask. When he puts it on, he changes from a bank clerk into a superhero in bright yellow clothes.

Carrey said the story line of the 1994 movie is similar to the book, *Dr. Jekyll and Mr. Hyde*. Asked who he is, Dr. Jekyll or Mr. Hyde, Carrey said, he's both. "I'm the meek, nice guy who might not say what he wants, and the crazy 'In Living Color' guy."

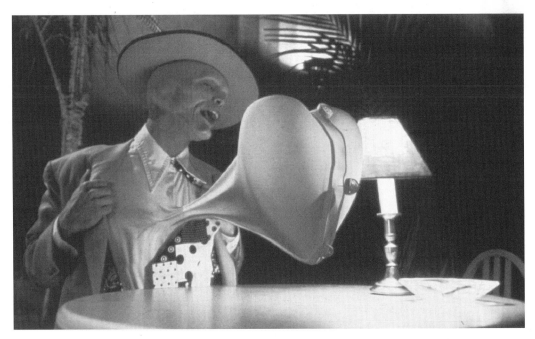

A scene from The Mask, *which used high-tech computer graphics.*

While filming *The Mask* in 1994, Carrey accepted an offer to costar in *Dumb and Dumber.* The studio paid him $7 million. That's the most money Carrey made for doing any TV show or movie. Asked what he's going to do with the money, Carrey said at the time that he had already spent it.

In *Dumb and Dumber*, Carrey played Lloyd Christmas who goes on a cross-country road trip with Harry Dunn, played by Jeff Daniels. The two are trying to return a briefcase of money to the owner. Cops, kidnappers, truck drivers, and anyone who happens to cross their path is met with misfortune.

Jim Carrey playing the mild-mannered Stanely Ipkiss in The Mask.

With his three movies making him a comedy star, Carrey's career was taking off. At the same time, however, he and his wife divorced. She didn't like the way his success was changing him, Carrey recalled. "Living with me these last couple of years has been like living with an astronaut," Carrey said of his success and marriage. "It's like, 'I just came back from the moon. Don't ask me to take out the garbage.'"

While filming *Dumber and Dumber*, Carrey met costar Lauren Holly. On the movie set, Carrey and Holly became friends and started dating. They later broke up and got back together again.

When *Dumb and Dumber* was released in 1994, it was a big hit at the box office. During the first weekend in theaters, the movie made $16.4 million. The movie remained number one for three weeks.

Jim Carrey (right) with Jeff Daniels in the hit comedy Dumb and Dumber.

MORE ADVENTURES

During 1994, Carrey talked freely with reporters about his career and his upcoming movies. Carrey said he loved working and that he might, in fact, work a little too much. "It's like a disease," Carrey said about not having much time to do other things. During his spare time, he promoted three new movies, including *Batman Forever* (in which Carrey plays the Riddler) and sequels to *Ace Ventura: Pet Detective* and *The Mask.*

In the spring of 1995, Carrey filmed *Batman Forever*. The most difficult part about playing the Riddler was learning how to spin a large question-mark-shaped cane. "It weighed, like, fifteen pounds," Carrey said. He hurt himself many times while trying to spin the Riddler's cane.

In January 1995, he turned down a role in a movie called *Thief of Santa Monica* even though he would earn $18 million. One newspaper said Carrey did not like the story.

When asked what he thought of his success, Carrey recalled his childhood. Without the many disappointments in his life, Carrey said, "I don't think I would feel like I deserve success."

Every once in awhile, Carrey admitted to thinking, "Ooh, what if they take it all away?" But even if he lost it all, Carrey said he could still go down to the comedy clubs and make people laugh. For him, that's what he likes the most.

TV SHOWS AND MOVIES
(1984-1995)

1984	The Duck Factory (TV Show)
1984	Finders Keepers
1985	Once Bitten
1986	Peggy Sue Got Married
1988	The Dead Pool
1989	Earth Girls Are Easy
1990	In Living Color (TV Show)
1991	Jim Carrey's Unnatural Act (Showtime)
1992	Doing Time on Maple Drive (TV Show)
1994	Ace Ventura: Pet Detective
1994	The Mask
1994	Dumb and Dumber
1995	Batman Forever
1995	The Mask II
1995	Ace Ventura: When Nature Calls

JIM CARREY'S ADDRESS

To send a letter to Jim Carrey, write to:

UTA

9560 Wilshire Boulevard

Fifth Floor

Beverly Hills, California 90212

If you want to receive a reply, enclose a self-addressed stamped envelope with your letter.